VERB ANIMATE

Poems and Prompts from Collaborative Acts

VERB ANIMATE
POEMS AND PROMPTS FROM COLLABORATIVE ACTS
by Heid E. Erdrich

Copyright © December 01, 2024 Heid E. Erdrich

No part of this book may be used or performed without written consent of the author, if living, except for critical articles or reviews.

Erdrich, Heid E.
2nd edition

ISBN 1st Edition: 978-1-949487-44-2
ISBN 2nd Edition: 978-1-949487-50-3
Library of Congress Control Number: 2024947847

Cover art by Jonathan Thunder
Cover design by Baonhia Xiong
Editing by Kris Bigalk
Interior design by Natasha Kane

Trio House Press, Inc.
Minneapolis
www.triohousepress.org

PRAISE FOR VERB ANIMATE

"Master of portals and keeper of good mischief, Heid E. Erdrich's Verb Animate generously lends us a kaleidoscopic vision of grand love and vibrant community."

—Tashia Hart, author of *Native Love Jams*

"Congratulations and miigwech to Heid E. Erdrich for sharing these journeys into collaboration—for once again expanding my awareness of my own dance with poetry—and for affirming that all true collaboration leads more deeply toward the Self."

—Mark Turcotte, author of *Exploding Chippewas*

"Verb Animate is a thousand heartful stories, memories, and impulses that swirl into a single brilliant river. Erdrich's words are medicine—give yourself up to these magnificent lines that call us to flow together."

—Mona Susan Power, author of *A Council of Dolls*

Scan to view artworks referenced in the book on Verb Animate's companion site

https://www.triohousepress.org/titles/verbanimate

TABLE OF CONTENTS

Verb Animate	3
Skins, Forms, Flows, Tones	4
Notes from Collaboration: Dance	8
The Cleansing After	10
Standing Animate	11
Zorro and the Boarding School: Five Poems for Flamenco	13
Nishiime	20
Star Women	22
Mino Miinikaan/Good Seeds	23
Listens and Follows Directions Poorly	26
The Invention of Time	27
They Invent Time	28
Lexiconography	30
Anaamiindim/In the Depths of a Body of Water	31
Many Stars	32
Recognize Voice	33
Ode' Miikana/Heart Line	35
Thin Skin	37
Kindred River	39
Poetry Installations	42
Ways of Water Wash Over	43
Poetry Service Announcement	46

Verb Animate

I don't know what makes me do it, say yes sometimes.

When asked to collaborate for the first time, a voice inside me asked "What even IS collaboration?" Meanwhile my chin nodded yes. I felt wanted, flattered, sure that I could do whatever the other artist wanted. I mean they asked me, right?

Who that first artist was, I don't recall. I just remember the glamor of being in her presence—it was a woman—and I had that feeling of the cool kids asking me to sit at their table. My inner middle-schooler yearned to be asked so long ago... and here she is, perpetually impressed when she gets asked.

At first, and long after I should have, I couldn't picture how a poet could do anything that would be useful to an artist. I just acted cool like, collaboration, yeah, I know about that.

At some point I found out that the phrase "We should collaborate" can be code for "I find your talent equal to mine and am saying this inviting thing right now, but ..." Sometimes that "but" implied ...but I have no specific intentions, at present. Sometimes it was ...but I want to drink your blood.

Sometimes I got the ask from someone who wanted to exploit my work for some kind of ethnic content they thought they lacked. Sometimes it was an experiment they had no intention of involving me in beyond what they could extract.

Most often though, I've had extraordinarily excellent luck. The ask has been the hand of friendship, of collegiality, of kinship that reaches me in a time when I meet another's energy, when I need to further explore common notions, political intentions, shared images and obsessions. When I say yes, that's when I am restless in the black and white world of paper and ink or pixels on screen. I say yes when I sense I am about to create beyond the page, when I want to put poetry into forms that reach different audiences.

Still, I should say no more often.

But I like to be asked.

Skins, Forms, Flows, Tones

What holds water in a drop
tension that holds humans in

between
their sweet skins

water holds us
her arms bays
tide of blood
beat so close
                just our skins
                between

home and ocean
inland sea
river just   between us
                just a beat
                between
who you are
who I am
who we are

We call our own way back
climb a liquid ladder
pour ourselves into
various and fluid forms

                Between
bluegreen bays
gray lakes
river feeding life into our bodies

We flow across continents
flow through peoples
one water no matter

our drift   the rifts
and rips of tides

Our skins vibrate   afire
concordant   a blood current   sounding
Just us

Just this skin between us

Skins   skin   kin   kindred
kind   red   kind
kin   skin

What holds water in a drop
tension that holds humans
between   their sweet skins

her arms bays
tide of blood
beat so close
          just our skins
          between

home and body of water
just   between us
          just a beat
          between
who you are
who I am
who we are

You wear your skin   no matter   where
you inherited   your tones   smooth

over structure of bone   anyone who
looked at you   would know   No

Your home of skin

warm cool   sleek   subtle shag of days
steam of work   sweat and regret   and inked to say

My skin's a story
you cannot guess
a history you cannot claim

Tones songs   forms to say
let me tell you   you won't know me
by my blue-black blurred   word that bled into fade
          no matter

My skin's a story
you cannot guess

My people made me
My water claims me

You cannot guess
I swim a liquid ladder
distance no matter   no home too far

Skins   skin   kin   kindred
kind   red   kind
kin   skin

Carry me across dry days

My skin   my own sweet home for water
beating blood of history

We water walking   we skins

"Skins, Forms, Flows, Tones" was written for "Skin(s)," which was performed by Rosy Simas Danse, 2016. I had met Rosy around 2010, after having known of her work for years. In 2013, Rosy choreographed a solo for "Artifact Traffic," a collaborative performance I directed at Intermedia Arts. A year later, Rosy engaged me as poet and curator to collaborate on "Skin(s)". I voiced sound for the production which was abstracted into a composition by Francois Richomme. I also created an exhibit to accompany the performance at select venues.

Try This: Write down all of your associations with skin. What images, places, sensations, ideas or concepts pop into your brain? Don't try to make sense, just flow through the river of associative word play. Relax. Repeat phrases when you hit a pause. Look back much later to see what you made.

Notes from Collaboration: Dance

I'm a woman who does not move for a living or enough or barely at all some days. A woman who could not be mistaken for a dancer. I am large and often made to feel uncomfortable about my size. I find it difficult to sit still on the floor and yet, in working with dance makers, I've sometimes found myself sitting on the floor in a circle with extremely limber folks who can really hold a pose. Yet, my comfort and discomfort as a human body is the tool I use most in collaborative work. In any work.

There's a lot for me to face in witnessing the creation of work based in the body. It is hard for me not to think of my own body. Listen to its pains and wants. Mostly though it makes me yearn to move and distracts me, so I imagine my own body in motion, in the pleasure of expression. Dance draws me in, stops my interior narration of the experience. It is a great pleasure to be taken so far outside my head. Dance draws me into my body even when I am still.

The challenge of this work daunts me. It is not that I have avoided physical themes in my writing, it is just that I was forced to forge a new and embodied role in my work with choreographers. I am a woman of words and their work is beyond words. In a black box theater or in a dance studio or off-stage, I become a verbal artist in a non-verbal art form. Whether I am suited for this work or not is the question that draws me and repels me at once. How is it that I have found myself working with choreographers not once, but several times? The answer begins, perhaps, in friendship rather than shared aesthetics. Perhaps I sense something we share that I cannot get in other ways, cannot reach in written ways. Or perhaps there's something in our different, but shared, Indigenous and Native being in the world that has drawn me to work most often with choreographer Rosy Simas.

Rosy comes from Seneca people and is a member of her nation, a heron clan woman, raised with Ojibwe as close as family. We became colleagues in the Minneapolis art scene. Her way of creating involves a process that, at first, I found surprisingly intellectual and weirdly verbal when compared to other choreographers that I had observed as they made dance works. The biggest surprise I found when I first started visiting choreographers in their studios was that we work from very different parts of our brains and yet we both use language to map our work. The vocabulary of movements has poetic qualities. I've heard Rosy build work with dancers on clipped words and prompts "curve, torque, imagination, bone, gut" even the word "sharknado" which made me stifle a laugh. But I do not take these things literally or expect them to add up to a representational or narrative performance of any kind. Not expecting a narrative or some metaphor that creates a movement toward a shared understanding is extraordinarily hard for me. And yet I recognize my own attempts to do something similar. In my own poems, I sometimes want to do what these dancers do. What would it mean for me to "work toward projection" or be "more spatial" or make it "internally generated" and have internal mean my actual insides?

Try This: Write several lines about how your body "writes." Think of how your hands, fingers, wrists, elbows, spine, gut, or butt contribute to the act of writing. Start with the phrase: my ankle writes… or pick another less obvious part of your body, rather than the eyes, brain, hands. We so often think we write with the heart or mind, but what about the rest of our physical selves?

The poem that follows, "The Cleansing After," and parts of the prose sections on dance were written during an immersive residency with Rosy Simas Danse as they made "Weave" in 2018–2019.

The Cleansing After

>   We're evidence of the crime – John Trudell

Rinsed clear in the tide   agitated
with coarse river sand

thrashed on rocks   tide-rinsed
clean of your stains

worn from the wash   we cleanse
grow thin   transparent   obvious as guts
and as blue

Our function no longer suspect   so obvious
We know   we scrub we agitate   we rub wrong

disturb   until our elemental blue
runs clear through

Dead we say   our way home   red dirt
we say words   of earth

names of land   cleansed   bleached
scrubbed soaked leached

still we remain
so gritty   so agitated

so turgid
our waters drain
                so very gray-blue

so   human so   woman so
clearly   so not   you

Standing Animate

When I draft a poem, I sometimes imagine it as coalescing from the tiniest matter into a being with a voice and movement. The poem comes together in a horizontal attitude—I put it down on paper—or with light as a facsimile of paper and it exists this way as long as it is forming. When it is nearly formed, when it is ready to be born, I print it out and stand it up. Eventually, I will stand up and read this poem to an audience or into a microphone to be recorded. Eventually the poem will move in the world. The poem will have its own life and will be voiced by others. The poem becomes. The poem goes on becoming.

That said, although I give them a life, I've never thought about my poems as children. My children stood themselves up. They have their own voices and ways of moving in the world. A poem is always becoming, in every iteration and with every voice that meets it, that reads it. That reader creates or co-makes with me in order to understand or speak the poem aloud. We come into a relationship, into collaboration in a way. Perhaps this is why collaboration with dancers, which at first terrified me, became easier. Dancers always seemed so able to project meaning or feeling without explaining anything. A poem or poet sometimes has to, or wants to, explain. I might have envied dance as a seemingly more immediate art than poetry, but instead I felt a kinship develop. Perhaps dance began to feel familiar and like poetry to me because the first choreographer I worked with was a Flamenco dancemaker. I learned from her, and the Spanish artists performing her work, that flamenco centered on poetry and that the poet didn't just lend their words to the work, they had a role in its making. It was a challenge and a joy to take that role.

Originally commissioned for Zorongo Flamenco Dance Theater in 2012, these following five poems are a response to a family story told by choreographer Susana Di Palma. In her story, an ancestor, an Ojibwe woman, had two daughters who were taken by her white husband and sent to a mission boarding school far from home. Although she walked more than 60 miles—in deep winter—to retrieve her daughters, the girls refused to return to their Ojibwe mother. Two generations later, a granddaughter's love created a dance to explore and heal a family rift.

In the poem series a girl watches Zorro on TV in the 1950's. When that girl grows up, she thinks of the story of her Ojibwe grandmother losing her daughters to a mission boarding school and walking a long way only to find they refused to come home. As an artist, she imagines a revised story where a hero like Zorro helps her family reunite and escape the crow-like nuns at the school.

Zorro means fox and the word for fox in Ojibwemowin is waagosh. Me-Me is an Ojibwe name for woodpecker. In the poem series, the woodpeckers or flickers for which Madeline Island in Wisconsin are named, call to and lead the characters home.

The final poems in this series, "Tricky" and "Parade at Noon Day" come from my interview with Susana Di Palma. She shared memories of her grandmother's dedicated Ojibwe spiritual practice and her difficulties adapting to the world of her Christian daughters when they were finally reunited with their mother as young adults. In my poetic imagining of the story, Naa'wakwe Gaabow (my translation of the name she wrote down for Susana) never stops believing her daughters and granddaughter will understand and respect her Ojibwe ways. Through her creation of "Zorro and the Boarding School: Five Poems for Flamenco," that is exactly what Susana Di Palma did.

Zorro and the Boarding School: Five Poems for Flamenco

WXYZ

She prints in black crayon—WXYZ—
letters for animals this kid has never met:
Z is for zebra, Y is for Yak.
A train wreck of little used consonants,
a pile up at the dead end of the alphabet—WXYZ.
Then Zorro slashes a Z
across the curved glass of her TV
and a deep unknown X
solves with a dark hero who could be
some kind of mixed blood, maybe,
some answer to all the words with W:
Who? What? When? Where?
And sometimes Y.

Walking the Frozen Road

Walking this frozen road,
I see waboose, the rabbit, on crusted snow,
calm in moonlight, not even a shiver
in the silver tips of its pelt.

I freeze through and think of you, Dear Ones.

Listen, through your dreams' singing
— that's the stars
who shattered into brilliance
in the black sky and grew still.

Listen, within that stillness: footsteps.
What else can a mother do, but come for you?

My dears, you must learn to be as waboose.
Rabbits who pose no threat.

Rabbits tense with energy,
then sprung like traps and tricky,
outwitting fox when he pounces.

Walking this frozen road, seeking you,
telling stories into your dreams...

Nights spark with speaking stars
and something in the moonlight:
fox, streak of warm silk aflame.

Walking this frozen road,
I see my two girls, my little rabbits,
grown white, grown still as snow,
cold in moonlight, not even a shiver,

no silver in their eyes.

Listen, within that stillness: footsteps.
What else can a mother do, but come for you?

Golden Woodpecker

Call me Me-Me and follow me,
though it's hollow, an echo
that leads you to the bay.

Flicker feathers, shafts of gold,
Your silver blade, her pounding,
on doors of iron wood.

Pounding Me-Me, Me-Me
follow my echoing,
all the way home.

Call me Me-Me and follow me,
though it's hollow, an echo
that leads you to the bay.

Flicker feathers, shafts of gold,
Your silver blade, my pounding,
pounding Me-Me, Me-Me
follow my echoing,
all the way home.

All the way,
follow me,
to the bay
and all the hollow way home.

Tricky

Trickier than I thought—
now I took up with the fox.

Sometimes the road veers off,
then flash-fur-fire and he's back,
and crows call crack-crack-crack.

Tricky woods, I could get lost,
track the tracker and I'm back.
We hunt waboose like that.

Waagosh fox and silk black crows
their shawls, his mask, that black.

Now I took up with fox:
gold eyes slant in his mask,
tips of black growing more black
a cape of crows flows from his back.

To take up with a fox!
Slick as whiskey— amber black.

Tricky woods, I could get lost
track the tracker and I'm back.
We hunt lost girls like that.

Waboose with rabbit tricks
keep us lone, lean as the moon.

Wagoosh fox and silk black crows
their shawls, his mask, that black.
Crows crack like black winged nuns.

Step to step, we walk, we walk.
when you take up with a fox.

Parade at Noon Day

for Naa'wakwe Gaabow

What a strange parade, this town.
Priest with rope-swinging robe
and white floats of saints in sashes,
the red and white and the blue and the cross.

Do you think I cannot see you?
My own girls, my white hares?
The moon follows you as I do.

Oh, my dears, his strange language fit into my ears
and I understood what you saw when I pounded
when they opened the huge wood and iron doors:
tree of crows,
slinking fox,
strange old woman
who stuttered with cold
in a language full of anger
in words you'd never heard.
No wonder you wouldn't come home.

What a strange parade I'm in here—
Priest with rope-swinging robe,
me tricked by whiskey and crow loud,
the fringe and the wings and the pelt and the flame.

Can you believe the fox means you no harm?
Can you believe he'll help you back, dears?
The moon stands at noon, to wait for you, as I do.

What a strange parade we make—
Fox with a black-swinging cape,
his black fur outlined smile, curl of tongue,
and the teeth, white as ice, and the moon at noon.
Oh, my dears, strange fox language fits into my mouth

that's what you see when I pound through town:
cape of crows,
slinking fox,
strange old woman
followed by the moon—
she stutters with anger
in words you've never understood.

It's a wonder how the moon waits,
as grandmothers wait, for years,

until our children's children come home.
Moon waits, it's a wonder, soon the dear ones come home.

Try This: Write about homecoming and its opposite, when someone does not return home—but not because that person died. Maybe they escaped, maybe the whole family left a home, maybe they found a home in another person—maybe that person was you?

Nishiime

Working with Zorango Flamenco was the first of many collaborations I engaged with artist and animator Jonathan Thunder. I am profoundly grateful to Jonathan, who created visual art related to these poems. His images were projected during the flamenco performance and it created an enchanting and slightly spooky stage that suited the production perfectly.

Not surprisingly, Jonathan's reputation has grown enormously in recent years. We don't get to work together often any more so I am thrilled to have Jonathan Thunder's artwork on the cover of this book. For me, working with Jonathan is magic and I am grateful. No matter what I dream up, he gets it. His distinct imagery holds tremendous power. Collaborating with Jonathan showed me enormous possibilities for poems in videographic forms. It changed the way I wrote on the level of line, use of white space, punctuation—everything.

One of the poems I wrote for Susan Di Palma became *Walking this Frozen Road*, an animated video which Jonathan made in 2017. I have collaborated with Jonathan on several videos, many of which you can see on my Vimeo and YouTube channels including the animated versions of "Ode' Miikana/ Heart Line," a poem included in this collection. Most of the videos Jonathan animated for me were created around my poems, but we also worked together on an Ojibwe language video "Gaa-ondinang dakawaanowed Makwa" or "How the Bear Got a Short Tail," directed by filmmaker Elizabeth Day.

I have come to think of both of these filmmakers, Jonathan and Elizabeth, as younger siblings, each is my nishiime, as we say in Anishinaabemowin. Much like my collaborations with Jonathan, working with Elizabeth has been amazing for me. The vibe, the synchronicity, the synergy, and all the other great things that come from our work together go beyond anything I could ever have wished for as a solitary poet. I sometimes sense the work I do with Anishinaabe artists reaches back to some shared ancestor we all have and makes their struggles worthwhile. We are here because they fought to exist as Ojibwe people, Anishinaabeg, and our art honors their survival.

Elizabeth has had great success as a documentary filmmaker and is currently working on her first feature-length film. I'm so grateful that Elizabeth and I were once able to have some creative fun together which resulted in several films on my own poems and on those of Louise Erdrich, my eldest sister. You can see these films on my Vimeo and YouTube channel, as well as on this book's companion website:

 http://www.triohousepress/titles/verbanimate.

Elizabeth and I also created a kind of documentary poem titled "Skin Frequencies." This project was part of community engagement for the Rosy Simas Danse production titled "Skin(s)." The video is a record of what identity and skin might have to do with one another. For the video, we interviewed dozens of Native people in four cities. In Chicago, Minneapolis, San Francisco and Oakland, California, we simply asked people two questions: 1) How do you identify? 2) What place do you feel connected to?

Elizabeth's gorgeous videography of the setting for each interview (at Indian centers, art galleries, outdoor community gatherings, and homes) and her openness as an editor allowed me to indulge some wacky poetic ideas that actually worked. The repetition in the film captures the rhythm I sensed in moving between four locations. The diverse appearances of those answering our question reveal that identity is anything but skin deep.

Try This: ask four people the same question and record their answers. Choose an open-ended question so they can't answer yes or no. Create a poem from their answers that uses four stanzas or stanzas composed of four lines or both. Ask yourself if the rhythm of four creates a story for you. It always does for me.

Star Women

The poem that follows, "Mino-minaanan/The Good Seeds" was created for Ananya Dance's production "Roktim: Nurture Incarnadine," 2015. The poem was danced by performer Reneé Copeland in the Twin Cities performance. In preparation to write this poem, I attended a workshop in which choreographer Ananya Chatterjea was developing the work with dancers. Rather than a rehearsal of dance moves, this gathering also engaged storytelling, relaxation exercises, and information on the historical events around protests in India involving women protecting seeds from corporations.

In writing for "Roktim: Nurture Incarnadine," for her dance company's website, Ananya explains how she thought of the environmental leaders Vandana Shiva and Wangari Mathai and "… the movements they lead—the Navdanya (nine seeds) farm, and the Green Belt movement—when they met." Ananya describes her research and creative process that "… made sure that we all realized the deep link of seeds, earth, and food to culture, indigenous knowledges, and self-determination of peoples." All of these notions were common to my thinking as I created my poem "Mino Miinikaan/Good Seeds" around a long-told story of Indigenous origins via a woman who fell from the stars bringing seeds with her to earth. A similar figure is pictured in Jonathan Thunder's image on the fly leaf of this book.

Try This: Write about a present or past political protest from the point of view of an archetypal figure. For example: Wonder Woman Against War On Gaza.

Mino Miinikaan/Good Seeds

testa-cotyledon-plumule-radicle-
seedcoat-seed-leaf-shoot-root

Hands in dark earth, we recall her
Or feel we can
the woman who first planted
the first planter
the mother of us all

This is an old story from everyone everywhere
       A woman and garden a fruit and a pit

Her heart a seed   she a woman split

life grew from it

Some seeds need fire to crack their code and grow
Some seeds require subtle cues
moisture seeping through husk

What engenders the seed breaks it
Elements bent on it in the dark
                      hot then wet then light
In the end the wind sends the pollen and we begin again

Earth swims in her hands
microbes, tiny animals, minerals,
full of life she feels –she fills

                      In a time of broken seeds
                            seeds sold broken

Earth swims in our hands
microbes, tiny animals, minerals,
full of life we feel –we fill

millions of living things in each handful
flooding our brains with earth praise
at the touch of loam, richness, fertile ground

This is an old story from everyone every where
        A woman and garden a fruit and a pit

Her heart a seed   she a woman split

life grew from it

Hands in rich earth, we recall her
Or feel we can
The woman who first planted,
then saved, these seeds

her cache pot buried in her homeland
Anishinaabeg homeland still

                            In a time of broken seeds
                                  seeds sold broken
testa-cotyledon-plumule-radicle
seedcoat-seed leaf-shoot-root

We have lost her name for this food
We call it Gete okosomin, the ancient seed

                            In a time of broken seeds
                                  seeds sold broken

Imagine what she would think
near a millennium later—
we grow it in our city gardens

                      In a time of broken seeds
                                      seeds sold broken

As we plant she planted—she is planting still

          The Good Woman falls from another world, clutches
          at roots and rocks and creatures as she tumbles.
          Her hair rains over her face. She does not know time.
          When she lands, in her pockets, in her hands,
          all medicines, minerals, seeds we will need,
          all that the people must know to survive.

This is an old story from everyone everywhere
        A woman and garden a fruit and a pit

Her heart a seed   she a woman split

life grew from it

As we plant, she plants

The heart splits
       the seed engenders
              we do not know time

Listens and Follows Directions Poorly

The above phrase was circled on my grade school report card a few times, along with "talks too much."

The following two poems are versions of the same poem. The first was written in response to a prompt to write about winter. The second prompt asked me to fit the digital space parameters of an illuminated highway sign of the kind that are used to direct traffic during construction. However, there actually was no first prompt. I had not listened or followed directions. I had started the assignment without looking at the instructions. Starting over was tricky, but I was determined to make a poem that was much the same as the first version—just shorter. These two versions,"The Invention of Time," and "They Invent Time" came out of Northern Spark's "Words for Winter: Illuminate South Loop"—a series of poems by several poets to be projected using traffic displays along the path of the light rail during the Super Bowl which Minneapolis hosted in 2018.

Try This: Draft a poem using no more than 10 characters (letters) per line. Spaces and all punctuation count as characters. Imagine this poem being displayed on a digital sign along a road. What do you want to say to folks using light? What do you want to say to people passing by if you can only say it in 2–3 second bursts?

The Invention of Time

Leave it to humans
lit as we are with brilliance
of the sort that flashes
in the dark cave of brain—

Take the Moon
in English with her OO
noon-sounding name.

Leave it to humans who name
all things seen and unseen—
all things guessed,
who name light and make it a place.

Take the Moon/Gokomis
in Anishinaabe with her OKO
grandmother-sounding name.

Leave it to women who name
all things seen and unseen—
all things understood,
who name light and make it time.

They Invent Time

Leave
it to
humans

lit w/
bright
thought

flashes
in the
cave

of brain

Moon in
English
her OO

noon
sound
name.

Leave it
2 humans
who name

all seen
all
unseen

all things
guessed

who
name
light

make it
a place.
Moon

Gokomis
in Ojibwe
w/her OKO

grandma
sound
name

Leave it
2 women
who name

all seen
all
unseen

all things
under
stood

who name
light &
make it

time.

Lexiconography

I created "Anaamiindim: In the Depths of a Body of Water" out of conversations with other Native women poets that we had in person and via email around the Water Protectors at Standing Rock. As a result, "Words for Water," a Whitney Museum performance for Standing Rock was performed by Natalie Diaz, Layli Long Soldier, Jennifer Foerester, composer and violinist Laura Ortman and others in 2017. I performed via phone. In addition, filmmaker Xiaolu created a poem video based on "Anaamiindim: In the Depths of a Body of Water," starring my fellow tribeswoman Inez Dakota in 2019. This poem was also published in Orion Magazine in 2018.

Both "Anaamiindim: In the Depths of a Body of Water," and "Many Stars" which follows, are in a form I call "lexiconography" that uses a dictionary as a prompt. It is, perhaps, a kind of found poem. I use this approach to relate to words in Anishinaabemowin, the Indigenous language of Ojibwe people that I study, but have not learned to speak well. These are poems of words sought and found in the "The Ojibwe People's Dictionary" (https://ojibwe.lib.umn.edu/).

Try This: Find a dictionary—doesn't have to be an English dictionary—and pick a page at random. Put each word on the page into a brief context or conversation with the previous word on the page to create a narrative or a series of images that resonate. It does not have to make sense at first. The idea is to play with the similar sounds of words presented in an alphabetical list. See what comes up.

Anaamiindim/In the Depths of a Body of Water

Bakobiikawe	S/he/they leaves tracks going into	the water
Bakobiidaabi'iwe	She/they dives into	the water
Bakobii	S/he/they goes down into	the water
Agwamo	S/he/they floats, still in	the water
Mookibii	S/he/they emerges from	the water
Gwaaba'ibi	S/he/they draws	the water
Biidoobii	S/he/they brings	the water
Nibi		the water

Many Stars*

for Jonathan Thunder

Ishpiming iwidi gegoo waawaasise   *There's something up in the sky flashing

Ishpiming   *the sky up high in heaven

anang   *star

anangokaa   *many stars
    there are (many) stars
    stars present abundant

Anishinaabekwe   *an Indian woman
    an Ojibwe woman
    a human woman

Oshkiniigikwewi   *s/he/they is a young woman
    first time woman

Mindimooyeniwi   *Old woman
    s/he/they is an old woman

Wiisaakodewikwe   *Metis woman
    a Native woman of mixed ancestry
    scorched wood woman

Ishkodewi   *s/he/they is a fire (of the sun)

Ishpiming iwidi gegoo waawaasise   *there's something up in the sky flashing

*A sought and found poem from the Ojibwe People's Dictionary, which is available online.

Recognize Voice

He called me out of the blue. We'd never met. We talked about animals indigenous to Minnesota for quite awhile before Christopher Lutter-Gardella asked me to collaborate on a public art project he hoped to create called "Wolf & Moose." He described his sculpture style and I imagined two huge creatures coming into being. They would be lit up and have audio powered by a stationary bike beneath each animal. The audio would be the words of a poem I would create to give context to the relationship between wolves and moose. Christopher was aware of the biological and environmental connection between the species, as was I, but I also knew there was an Ojibwe star story about wolf and moose. Star stories can be in the category of stories considered alive and not to be told when there's no snow on the ground. I turned to Ojibwe artist Carl Gawboy, who contributed to "Ojibwe Sky Star Map Constellation Guide," to get me a sense of what I was allowed to say about the cosmology related to wolves and moose. Eventually we got permission to use images based on those in the book in an animation by Jonathan Thunder.

"Wolf & Moose," composed of pre-consumer waste and partly made by community volunteers, were installed in the park across from the convention center in downtown Minneapolis. Each animal, pelts made of window screen material and plastic waste, looked uncannily alive and could be made to open their mouths and wag their heads when visitors tugged on ropes. Lights and sound were activated when passersby pedaled the bikes under each sculpture. They created a carnival air in an otherwise dark park. I stopped by many times while they were installed and once a woman who I had seen there often—there were many people who essentially lived in the park—bounded up to me to show me how to activate the sculptures. She had become a kind of docent of "Wolf & Moose," explaining to people what to do with the bikes, cautioning them not to climb or tug too hard on the ropes. When we began talking she cried out, "It's YOU—the voice!" and leapt into my arms.

As Christopher Lutter-Gardella and I collaborated on his Creative City Challenge winning sculptures, I began a parallel video collaboration with animator Jonathan Thunder and poet-composer Trevino Brings Plenty. The animated version of "Ode' Miikana/Heart Line" exists in two versions: one autotunes my voice to a wolf and one autotunes it to a moose. Trevino had been experimenting with autotune as a way to point out the dreaded "poet voice," the ubiquitous manner in which many American poets perform that creates a sing-songy quality I wished to avoid. Autotune was an experiment and a lesson in understanding my own voice through technical manipulation. Turns out that my speaking voice tone was actually quite close to the moose whose audio I had captured from publicly available sources. It was a male moose. Humph.

Ode' Miikana/Heart Line

Always following, that one, always trailing.
Ma'iingan Miikana, the wolves' path, in stars.

Our first teacher, Ma'iingan, brother,
the wolf. Always following, that one,
always trailing. Now you follow, too.

Our hearts align—
What happens to one happens to the other.

Ode' Miikana, Ma'iingan Miikana.
Heart Path. Wolf Trail. Star way.

Through Gaagige-giizhig, Forever Sky,
The Animate Universe. Now we animate.

Ecliptic, Ma'iingan Miikana,
Wolf Trail, trailing moose, mooz

through Jiibay Ziibi, River of Souls,
The Milky Way, the way
we humans know all it is we know.

Know Mooz, sister who gave all
to humans, Anishinaabeg.

You follow, too. You make a way.
Mooz-Ma'iingan. Moose-Wolf.

Our hearts align—
What happens to one happens to the other.

Ode' Miikana, Ma'iingan Miikana.
Heart Path. Wolf Trail. Star way.

Through Gaagige-giizhig, Forever Sky,
The Animate Universe. Now we animate.

Overhead that one follows
Summer to Fall, Niibin—Dagwaagin.

Keep on the move to find Mooz.
You follow, too. You make a way.

What happens to one happens to the other.

Twin to Ma'iingan, Wolf Brother,
Our first teacher—your trail across our sky,

We were pitiful, Ma'iingan, then you showed us
the way to Mooz, sister who gave—everything.
Food, clothes, sleds, shoes, tools. All we need to survive.

Our hearts align—
What happens to one happens to the other.

Ode' Miikana, Ma'iingan Miikana.
Heart Path. Wolf Trail. Star way.

Through Gaagige-giizhig, Forever Sky,
The Animate Universe. Now we animate.

Thin Skin

In 2023, I was asked to write a poem to be animated by artist Moira Villiard for projection on a building. I wrote the poem, shared the text, and recorded my voice. We discussed the project once, very briefly. Weeks later, it was exciting to see Moira's visual language in response to my words. Although we never discussed it, many of the same images, in the same style, were playing in my mind as I wrote. The resulting video was projected on the enormous library edifice in downtown St. Paul as part of Wakpa Triennial, a public art festival that involved many Dakota and Ojibwe artists.

Since my work on the project was virtual and I did not have a lot of time in which to complete the poem I decided to use associative writing to create it. I wrote the images, associations and concepts that first came to mind after reading Moira's concept for the film: Kinship. She defined kinship as both by blood and relationship and she made clear kinship might be harmful as well as nurturing. I associate kinship with a river, the blood that flows through me, a red river. The Red River of the North flowed below the hospital room where I was born. My mother's people have lived along the Red River for hundreds of years—long before white people arrived to straighten it and cause it to flood. In my poem "Kindred River," the flow of associations starts in my origin place.

What lives near a river and is thin-skinned? I let my flow of associations extend from river to frog through the notion of kin and skin. To me, raised as a light-skinned Ojibwe woman with a large extended family, the idea of skin was always confused in the word kin. My kin are both darker and lighter skinned. I have always been aware of the way skin color disadvantages some of my relatives. Along with its privilege, being lighter created distance from my kin that has its own, lesser difficulties. Being a sensitive poet of a child, I was often told not to be thin-skinned about any teasing or to toughen up. In many ways I did toughen up, for better or worse.

Working on Moira's project reminded me of collaborating on Rosy Simas's dance project "Skin(s)." In considering skin and kinship, I centered on vulnerability in both my poem for Moira and my poem for Rosy.

Try this: Think of a word that has two or more meanings and examine the way each word is used by writing about a body of water. Right River, for instance or Tear Lake.

Kindred River

When we say familiar
We don't mean only family

Slow flow grown suddenly red
Daybreak or nightfall—that glow

Or a noon view of brown current
Green waters in swirl and drift

What makes us inhale wet scent of
grass and mud—Genetic memory?

We've never been here
Smells so familiar though

We say blood to mean related
We say blood to say ancestor

When we say familiar
We don't mean only family

When we say family
We don't mean biology

Even if all we get is biology
When we say biology

We might think of frogs
Not frogs green on a lily

Not the low song along
The river on spring nights

We might think of splayed frogs
We might think of high-school

When we say family

We don't mean biology

We say blood to mean related
We say blood to say ancestor

It's a red river—a fine line
What we mean by relationship

What we mean by relations
Means kin and skin

We can be thin-skinned as frogs
Dissect relationship but still relate

When we say familiar
We don't mean only family

We say blood to mean related
We say blood to say kin

Kindred spirits too
Red waters within us all

Kind waters we need you
We all do—all of us related

Related by water we need
Water for All my relations

Indinawe maaganidoog
Familiar phrase we will say

To say We are all related
Indinawe maagonidoog: we kin

We will be kin and kind as water
Red water flows through us all

Familiar, kindness in us
Kind red river forever

Kindred river forever

Poetry Installations

My sense of the whole of my poems has a lot to do with the way poems look on the page. I think of some poems as sculptures built of words. Each black letter I type has a specific weight that I sense and punctuation weighs even more. There is no other way to put it, my poems feel like sculptures to me. I build them.

It has been a great experience to have my poems treated as visual art. I installed "Anaamiindim: In the Depths of a Body of Water," at SooVAC gallery in Minneapolis in 2019 as a part of my contribution to "Skew Lines," a dual artist exhibition with Rosy Simas. A year later, "Ways of Water, Wash Over" was commissioned and installed in "A Shared Body," a group exhibition at Florida State University, Tallahassee in 2020. The title of the exhibition was taken from this poem. The poem itself was partially composed during my residency in Tallahassee with Rosy Simas Danse. The text "Ways of Water, Wash Over" follows here as the final poem in Verb Animate.

Ways of Water Wash Over

We wade and dive
                         we stroke and ripple ponds
                                 and pools as if we grew there

                      We did grow there   in her wash and wonder

We go deep as if   we know the ways of water
                         we knew water longer
                                than this dry life
We beat with water long before we landed
                             in our mother's hands
                                 long before we first
              cried out at the heaviness of air
                     and mourned the loss of a shared body
         its waters our waters
                          our original atmosphere

She washes over all

            we give in to her tug   alive flow directed   current of now

We think we know the ways of water

but does that current drag us back
                     or course us forward
                               wash us to a future?

                                 The future we wish for her
                                 future we wish of her
                                 future awash with her

We tangle in the wash and wake
                along the sea or lake or river

We think we know her ways

        but does she take us in
            or do we go along with water?

    We give ourselves to her tug   current now   how we stand for her
          now the women walk for her   bear her along awhile
                    her own flow   always back to water
Even leaving she flows back
      her currents and waves here
            then gone   inconstant yet
                          consolation

        Our eyes desire
     the water view   the earth's rim
       outlined by her blue
            that is not her blue   borrowed sky
              but still she washes over all

Drawn to her shore   she goes indigo and greens and tips like a bowl

        pours toward me a last hope

says NO she will not be sold or bored through or slowed with silt or bottled up
her rage not for sale   now we see she's stolen   still she washes

Her nature to make us forget   smooth like sand
        forget what it was we so wanted
            what we so needed that we'd take it
                    from her   take her

On her shore you see
                she sees us too and all we've done
dirt or virtue means nothing to her   she washes over all

    We carry her   we care for her
        we export her we usurp her we sell her

we hardly see her we don't know her
                        We all seem the same to her
                                          so she'll wash over all

she'll wash over all   wash over all   over all   all

Poetry Service Announcement

When I came to live in the Twin Cities in 1992, I soon met Native artists and writers through the Native Arts Circle in Minneapolis. Through the work of Juanita Espinoza, Mona Smith, and Ernie Whiteman, I heard stories of Bde Óta Othúŋwe. In three decades of listening to Dakota, Ojibwe, Ho Chunk and other Native artists, I have come to know this place. A little.

Having grown up spending a great deal of time in Chahinkapa Park, once a Dakota village, far from the Turtle Mountain Reservation where I am enrolled, I have always felt drawn to places long important to Indigenous people. In the case of my home town, Wahpeton, North Dakota, the people are the Sisseton-Wahpeton Oyate. So I knew to listen carefully when I came to the Twin Cities. Ever since, I've studied, supported, worked with, and learned from Native artists and organizations working to renew sacred relationships to land or to place. I learned from place by simply, with awareness, being in place. Now I have asked other poets to join me in writing poetry by learning from place.

I have spent the past year, 2024, serving as the inaugural Minneapolis Poet Laureate. A big reason I applied for and engaged my position as poet laureate is that I see great potential in collaborative acts across sectors as a means to creating civil understanding and commitment to our city's future.

I planned and engaged in a project I called Poetry Service Announcement or PoeSA. Through PoeSA, I commissioned Minneapolis poets to write about places important to Dakota and other Native people who have a long history and presence in the city. I did so because it is important to recognize this place exists in its own right. This place, known as Bde Óta Othúŋwe has, for millions of years, held the lives of uncounted plants and creatures, it has experienced climate cataclysm, risen and fallen with powerful waters, birthed cultures, and has been home and origin place to Indigenous people since time immemorial. Bde Óta Othúŋwe has also welcomed immigrants, refugees, and all who sleep under stars that once shone far to the south in our hemisphere.

This land and water and sky also suffer disruption and abuse. Now there's growing hope for recovery and renewal through the collaborative efforts of Native-led organizations that are restoring original place names, planting and returning indigenous species to original habitats, surfacing waters channeled into sewers and restoring the falls, Owamni Yomni, to the sacred relationship the Dakota hold with it.

These efforts expand from parks and public projects to art and cultural efforts. In acknowledging these ongoing aspects of renewal, PoeSA works with youth through elder-aged Minneapolitans who are BIPOC and Native, poets from justice-impacted communities or refugees of genocide, to create poems around the idea of Indigenous place. I have long held that if Minneapolis thought of itself indigenously, as originating and existing exactly where the place itself wills us to be, we might value our community, well, communally. In unity. We may seem like a people easily divided, but we are not. We are all called to be here, drawn here, or we did not have a choice but we remain here, together. It is a miracle we are all here at once in a place Dakota people know as the birthplace of humanity. What if we are here because of this very place? This earth, this water, this sky—these lakes, rivers and gathering places that hold us.

Even as it considers the Indigenous history and presence of this place, PoeSA also looks to the future in promoting poetry as public art. Much like the projects I engaged to create the poems in this book, PoeSA creates conversations around the possibilities for poetry beyond the page and stage: poetry as art installation, in film and within public art. Through PoeSA my hope is that work as a writer and as the Poet Laureate will be amplified through support of other Minneapolis poets' future projects and collaborations.

I have come to know Bde Óta Othúŋwe, Minneapolis. A little. It is through the generosity of artists and culture bearers that I know the little I do and have begun to think of this place as a relative. I am grateful. I am at home.

This book is dedicated to the holistic notion that all the gifts Bde Óta Othúŋwe gives us come through a collaborative and co-creative spirit.

Acknowledgments

The poems and prose works in this collection were created as commissions or as my contributions to collaborations with other artists. Although made public through interdisciplinary performances and installations, most of these works have not been printed in publications with the exception of: "Anaamiindim: In the Depths of a Body of Water," Orion Magazine, 2018; and, "The Invention of Time," The Rumpus, 2018. Specific previous use of these works in public are acknowledged within the body of this publication. In each case copyright is retained by Heid E. Erdrich. Poems contained here sometimes appeared in earlier versions that have been slightly altered for this publication.

I am grateful to my collaborators, who put my words in front of a broader audience than a poet usually meets. Thank you to Susana Di Palma, Jonathan Thunder, Rosy Simas, Elizabeth Day, Louise Erdrich, Angie Erdrich, Aza Erdrich, Rita Erdrich, Christopher Lutter-Gardella, Andrea Carlson, the late Jim Denomie and all the visual artists, dancers, choreographers, sculptors, curators, activists, poets, filmmakers, and other creators and performers who make my brain go pow! I could write without your inspiration, but I wouldn't want to, no how.

Loving thanks to my spouse John Burke and my family who helped me complete the final draft of this book while I was recovering from breaking both elbows and a wrist. T-Rex can't cut and paste.

I am grateful to Trio House Press staff and to my collaborators.

About the Author

Heid E. Erdrich is author of seven collections of poetry. Her honors include a National Poetry Series award, Native Arts and Cultures Foundation Fellowship, Loft-McKnight Fellowship in Prose, Minnesota State Arts Board grants, and two Minnesota Book Awards. Heid edited the anthology New Poets of Native Nations. Her poetry collection, Little Big Bully won the Rebekah Johnson Bobbitt National Prize for Poetry from the Library of Congress. Heid grew up in Wahpeton, North Dakota with a German American father, an Ojibwe and Metis mother, and six siblings. Heid is Ojibwe, enrolled in the Turtle Mountain Band of Chippewa. An independent scholar and curator, Heid is the inaugural Minneapolis Poet Laureate, for 2024. She is the James Welch Distinguished Visiting Professor at the University of Montana, Missoula in 2025. Her book Boundless: Abundance in Native American Art and Literature, co-authored by Lisa M. Crossman, is forthcoming in 2025.

About the Artist

Jonathan Thunder (b. 1977)

Thunder infuses his personal lens with real-time world experiences using a wide range of mediums. He is known for his surreal paintings, digitally animated films and installations in which he addresses subject matter of personal experience and social commentary. Jon is an enrolled member of the Red Lake Band of Ojibwe, and makes his home and studio in Duluth, MN.

He has attended the Institute of American Indian Arts (IAIA) in Santa Fe, NM and studied Visual Effects and Motion Graphics in Minneapolis, MN at the Art Institute International. His work has been featured in many states, regional, and national exhibitions, as well as in local and international publications. Thunder is the recipient of a 2020-21 Pollock – Krasner Foundation Award for his risk taking in painting. Since his first solo exhibit in 2004, he has won several awards for his short films in national and international competitions. His work is in the permanent collections of Museums and Universities.

https://www.jonthunder.com/

About the Art

Jonathan Thunder's painting on the cover of this book is titled "Night Whistler's Mother" (2024). It was originally created in six panels that total approximately 6' by 4'. It is installed at the University of Minnesota–Duluth.

The QR code image of Heid E. Erdrich in this book is based on a digital portrait by Jonathan Thunder as is Jonathan's self portrait accompanying his biography. Both were created in 2015.

Artist Statement

I grew up reading Mad Magazine, collecting Garbage Pail Kids, riding skateboards with elaborate, odd designs on the deck, listening to Public Enemy, Rage Against Machine, Tom Waits and watching MTV. The Twin Cities is my hometown, but I was born on the Red Lake Indian Reservation, home to the Red Lake Band of Ojibwe. These two worlds are integrated to me, yet far apart. Both worlds inform my perspective, my work, and my outlook to the future.

Interpretive figures representing identity, situations and socio-political commentary are often the leaping point for my imagery.

About the Book

Verb Animate was designed at Trio House Press through the collaboration of:

Kris Bigalk, Lead Editor
Natasha Kane, Supporting Editor and Interior Design
Baonhia Xiong, Cover Design
Jonathan Thunder, Cover Art

The text is set in Seria Sans Pro

About the Press

Trio House Press is an independent literary press dedicated to discovering, publishing, and promoting books that enhance culture and the human experience. Trio House Press adheres to and supports all ethical standards and guidelines outlined by the CLMP. For further information, or to consider making a donation to Trio House Press, visit us online at triohousepress.org.

www.ingramcontent.com/pod-product-compliance
Lightning Source LLC
Chambersburg PA
CBHW060542080526
44586CB00012B/823